Travel Through Brazil

Joe Fullman

QED Publishing

First published in the UK in 2007 by
QED Publishing
A Quarto Group company
226 City Road
London EC1V 2TT

www.qed-publishing.co.uk

A catalogue record for this book is available from the British Library.

ISBN 978 1 84538 659 7

Written by Joe Fullman
Designed by Chhaya Sajwan (Q2A Media)
Editor Honor Head
Picture Researcher Sujatha Menon (Q2A Media)

Publisher Steve Evans
Creative Director Zeta Davies
Senior Editor Hannah Ray

Printed and bound in China

Picture credits

Key: t = top, b = bottom, m = middle,
l = left, r = right, FC = front cover

Carsten Reisinger/ **Shutterstock**: 4t, **Index Stock Imagery**/ **Photolibrary**: 4 background,
17t, **Imagestate Ltd**/ **Photolibrary**: 6b, Jose Miguel Hernandez Leon/ **Shutterstock**: 7t,
Workbook, Inc./ **Photolibrary**: 7b, John Pennock/ **Lonely Planet Images**: 8b, **Oxford Scientific
Films**/ **Photolibrary**: 9t, 12t, 12b, Celso Pupo/ **Shutterstock**: 9b, **Animals Animals / Earth
Scenes**/ **Photolibrary**: 15t 10m, 13b, **Jtb Photo Communications Inc**/ **Photolibrary**: 10b,
14, 16b, 20t, 22b, 23b, **HYPERLINK** "http://www.alexrobinsonphotography.co.uk" **www.
alexrobinsonphotography.co.uk**: 15t, Viviane Moos/**CORBIS**: 15b, David Katzenstein/**CORBIS**: 17b,
Ricardo Azoury/**CORBIS**: 19t, Marcos Issa/**Argosfoto**: 19b, **Robert Harding Picture Library Ltd**
/ **Photolibrary**: 21t, 26–27t, John Maier Jr/ **Lonely Planet Images**: 21b, 22t, **popperfoto.com**: 25t,
Photo Researchers, Inc./ **Photolibrary**: 26b, **Peter Arnold Images Inc**/ **Photolibrary**: 27b.

Words in **bold** can be found in the glossary on page 31.

Contents

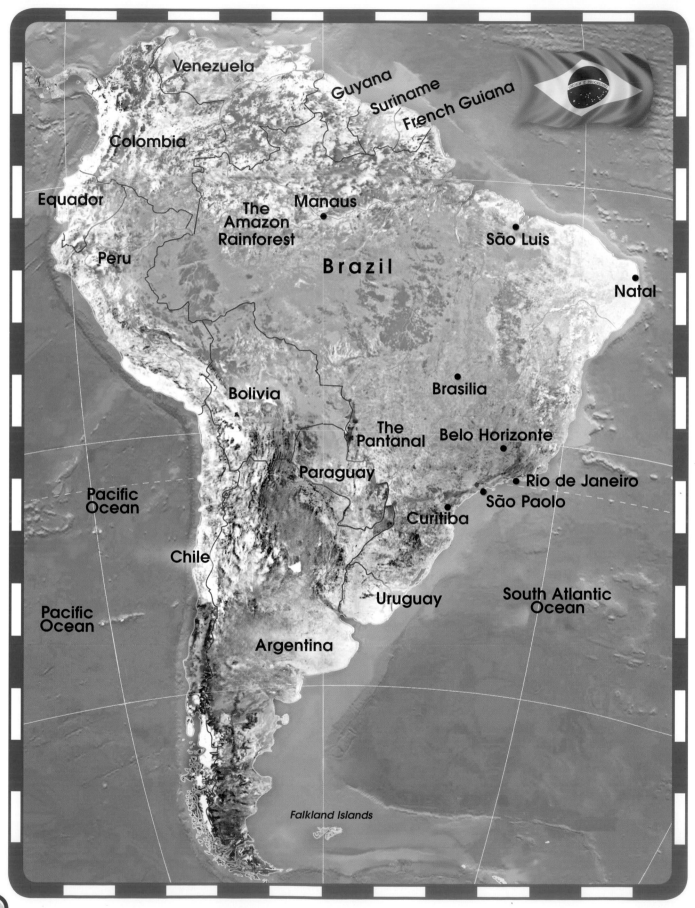

Venezuela

Guyana

Suriname

French Guiana

Colombia

Equador

Manaus

The
Amazon
Rainforest

São Luis

Peru

B r a z i l

Natal

Bolivia

Brasilia

The
Pantanal

Belo Horizonte

Paraguay

Rio de Janeiro

São Paolo

Pacific
Ocean

Curitiba

Chile

Uruguay

South Atlantic
Ocean

Pacific
Ocean

Argentina

Falkland Islands

Where in the world is Brazil?

Brazil lies on the **continent** of South America. It is bordered to the east by the Atlantic Ocean, and to the north, west and south by ten other countries. Brazil is South America's largest country and the fifth-largest country in the world. It also has the world's fifth-largest population, with over 180 million people. Most of these people live in large cities in the south-east of the country.

Did you know?

OFFICIAL NAME: Federative Republic of Brazil

LOCATION: South America

SURROUNDING COUNTRIES: French Guiana (a province of France), Suriname, Guyana, Venezuela, Colombia, Peru, Bolivia, Paraguay, Argentina, Uruguay

SURROUNDING SEAS AND OCEANS: North Atlantic Ocean, South Atlantic Ocean

LENGTH OF COASTLINE: 7367km

CAPITAL: Brasilia

AREA: 8 511 918sq km

POPULATION: 183 886 700

LIFE EXPECTANCY: Male: 68 Female: 76

RELIGION: Christianity (Catholicism)

LANGUAGE: Portuguese

CLIMATE: Cool in the far north, **tropical** in the north, centre and south-east, **temperate** in the south

HIGHEST MOUNTAIN: Pico da Neblina (2994m high)

MAJOR RIVER: Amazon (6540km long)

CURRENCY: Real (plural reais)

What is Brazil like?

Brazil is the biggest country in South America, taking up almost half of the continent. You could fit all of the countries of Europe inside Brazil. It has a coastline that stretches for thousands of kilometres and which includes some of the most amazing beaches in the world. Brazil also has a large population. There are more people living in Brazil than there are in the UK, France and Germany put together.

Rivers, rainforest and wildlife

Travelling around Brazil, you will see many long rivers. The longest is the mighty River Amazon, which flows through the northern half of the country. It contains more water than any other river on Earth. The Amazon flows through thick, wet **rainforest** which stretches for many thousands of kilometres. Over a quarter of the world's animals and plants live in the Amazon rainforest, including parrots, monkeys and large cats called jaguars.

The Amazon River flows through the rainforest in a series of long bends known as meanders.

Who lives there?

Many different peoples have made their home in Brazil over the years. The first people to settle here **migrated** from North America several thousand years ago. They are known as **indigenous** peoples or Amerindians. In the 1500s their land was conquered and taken over by invaders from Portugal, in Europe, which is why the national language of Brazil is Portuguese. People from all over the world now live here and over 60 per cent of Brazil's population is **mixed race**.

Rich and poor

Rich people and poor people in Brazil lead very different lives. The rich, who own most of the country's land, live in large, comfortable houses and often have servants. Brazil's poorest people live in **slums** known as favelas. Here, there is often no running water, electricity or sewerage system.

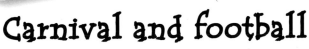
The slums, or favelas, of Rio de Janeiro are made up of hundreds of tiny shacks.

Carnival and football

Brazil is known throughout the world for its carnivals, when thousands of people fill the streets to sing and dance. Many performers in costumes parade through the streets of the city of Rio de Janeiro. As well as carnivals, Brazil is famous for its football team, which is thought by many to be the best in the world. It has won the **FIFA World Cup** five times, more than any other country.

People dress up in colourful costumes for a carnival.

Different climates

Brazil is a huge country. If you travelled all the way from the tip of north Brazil to the tip of south Brazil, you would have covered over 3000km and experienced lots of different climates.

Rain, rain, rain

The far north of Brazil is a mountainous **region**. When you travel here you will need to wear warm clothes, as the climate can be very cool. Temperatures get hotter as you head south into the Amazon rainforest, which is very warm and very wet all year round. The forest gets over two metres of rain a year – over five times as much as London or New York. Be sure to bring some waterproof clothing when travelling here!

Birds called egrets often live with herds of cattle in Brazil. They feed on small insects on the cows' skin.

Northern Brazil has many high, rocky mountains.

Hot Highlands

Heading further south from the rainforest, you reach the Brazilian Highlands. This area is still very hot, but is much less **humid** than the rainforest – you can take off your raincoat! Much of the land here is covered in grass where farmers keep cattle. To the west of this region is the Pantanal, an enormous area of **swamp land**. This is home to a large amount of wildlife, including alligators, giant otters and capybara, the biggest rodents in the world.

The Pantanal swamp is bigger than the whole of the UK.

Truly tropical

Most people in Brazil live in the south-east, which has a tropical climate. There is a wet season from October to March, when it rains almost non-stop, and a dry season from April to September. Many tourists visit this part of Brazil during the dry season to enjoy its beach **resorts**. The south of Brazil has hot summers and cold winters. Sometimes it even snows in winter.

I live in Belo Horizonte in the south-east of Brazil where it is hot most of the time. Even when it rains, it is still very warm. Next week, my family is going to visit my grandparents who live in Curitiba, which is over 750km south-west of here. Curitiba is much colder in winter than where we live. Mum says I will need to pack lots of jumpers to keep warm. She says that temperatures in Curitiba can go lower than 0°C, and that when it gets this cold, the water in ponds freezes over. I'm hoping that it might snow as I've never seen snow before.
Lucas

Rio de Janeiro's Copacabana beach is often filled with people sunbathing.

The long river

If you followed the Amazon River from where it starts in the Andes Mountains to where it pours into the sea on the Brazilian coast, you would have travelled over 6540km – that's longer than the distance from the USA to the UK across the Atlantic Ocean. The Amazon is the second-longest river in the world (after the Nile in Africa) and for much of its length it is surrounded by jungle. However, in some areas people live beside the river, farming the land and using boats to fish in the river's waters. Manaus is the largest city on the banks of the Amazon.

The Amazon has over 5000 **species** of fish – more than anywhere else in the world.

People who live in Manaus, on the banks of the Amazon, often use ferries to get around.

Not one river but many

As the Amazon makes its way to the sea it is joined by dozens of other streams and rivers, some over 1000km long. These are known as **tributaries**. The Amazon Basin, the name given to the area feeding water into the Amazon River, is ten times larger than France. The river provides a home to huge numbers of animals, including piranhas, a type of fish with razor-sharp teeth, and anacondas, which are the largest snakes in the world.

Wide and narrow

The Amazon River isn't the same size or shape all the way along. Where it begins in the steep mountains, it is thin and fast-flowing, with waterfalls and tumbling streams. As it reaches flatter ground, the river slows down and widens out. In some places the river is so wide that if you stood on one bank you wouldn't be able to see the bank on the other side. In some places the water runs almost clear, in other places it is cloudy with **silt**. The mouth of the Amazon, where the river meets the ocean, is absolutely enormous, measuring over 330km across – that's the distance from London to Paris.

Here you can see where the dark water of the Rio Negro river joins the lighter-coloured water of the Amazon.

Anacondas kill their prey by wrapping their bodies around them in tight coils.

I live in the city of Manaus on the banks of the Amazon River. The river plays an important part in my family's life. My father has a job as a tour guide, taking foreign visitors on fishing trips out on the river. They usually try to catch peacock bass, a very large fish that can grow more than a metre long and weigh over nine kilograms. My father also catches fish for our family to eat. Each morning he takes me to school in his boat.
Pedro

The vast forest

Brazil has the world's largest stretch of rainforest. In total it covers over a billion hectares of land. This huge jungle provides a home to more animals and plants than any other environment on Earth – over 1000 species of birds, over 40 000 species of plants, and more than a million species of insects.

Some Amerindian peoples hunt by using blowpipes and darts tipped with poison.

People of the rainforest

Around 200 000 Amerindians live deep in the rainforest. Their lifestyle has not changed much in hundreds of years. They hunt animals, and eat fruit and berries.

Good for everyone

Rainforests have many benefits to offer people. Rainforest plants produce huge amounts of oxygen for us to breathe and their leaves soak up **carbon dioxide**, which can cause **global warming**. Trees also help to keep the jungle soil in place. If the trees weren't there, the soil would be washed away by the rains and the land would be turned into desert. Most importantly, many modern medicines are made from rainforest plants. These include rosy periwinkle, which is used in a medicine to treat **leukaemia**.

Future of the rainforest

Brazil's rainforest is big, covering half the country, but it is not as big as it once was. A lot of trees have been cut down to provide timber and to clear land for farming. More will be cut down in the future. People worry that the loss of the rainforest will lead to **climate change** and the **extinction** of plant species that could have been used to make new medicines. Many **conservation groups** around the world **campaign** for the preservation of Brazil's rainforest.

Parts of the Amazon rainforest are very thick and can be difficult for people to travel through.

I live in a village deep in the forest. We get most of the food we need from the jungle, picking fruits and hunting animals. To make extra money, my father collects **açai** berries and Brazil nuts from the jungle and sells them at a nearby town. The people in my village are always careful not to hurt the forest, and only take the amount of food we need, so that there will always be food for tomorrow.

Tania

Crowded cities

Most Brazilians live in cities. Brazil has 13 cities with a population of over a million people. The country's three biggest cities, São Paolo, Rio de Janeiro and Belo Horizonte, are all in the south-east and are very crowded. If you walk around the centre of a Brazilian city, you will see many skyscrapers where people work. The houses are smaller in the **suburbs**, where many people live. In Brazil's warmer areas, houses are made of wood, which keeps them cool when the weather is warm. In the south, where the winters are cold, houses are made of brick to keep in the heat.

In Brazil there is a big gap between rich and poor. Over 80 per cent of the land is owned by under 5 per cent of the population.

The cathedral in Brazil's capital city, Brasilia, has a very unusual shape.

YOU'VE GOT MAIL

Many thousands of Brazil's poorest children have no family, no home, no money and don't go to school. They are called 'street children' and they survive by begging, stealing and scavenging rubbish. They sleep on the streets. When I grow up I will try to do something to help them.
Love Larissa x

São Paolo & Brasilia

São Paolo is Brazil's biggest city. Over 11 million people live here, making it the biggest city in the whole of South America. It is also Brazil's main **industrial** centre and has many factories. This is where the country's car industry is based. Despite its large size, São Paolo is not Brazil's capital. Rio de Janeiro, on the south-east coast, used to be the capital, but 50 years ago the people of Brazil decided that there were too many cities on or near the south-east coast. They decided to build a new city in the centre of the country which would be their capital. They called this new capital Brasilia. It is not very old, so it is not as large as many other Brazilian cities, but is growing more and more crowded.

There are many skyscrapers in the centre of São Paolo.

Industry and farms

The south-east is by far Brazil's richest region. Here you will find the biggest cities, the main industries and the best farms. The north is Brazil's poorest area. There are few industries and cities here and most people work on large **plantations**. Most of the land here is owned by a few rich landowners.

Traffic jams are common in Brazil's busy city streets.

Rio de Janeiro

Rio de Janeiro, on Brazil's south-east coast, is one of the world's most famous cities. It is also one of the largest cities in South America. The name, Rio de Janeiro, means 'River of January' in Portuguese, although many people call the city by the shorter name of 'Rio'. It is also often called 'A Cidade Maravilhosa', which means 'The Marvellous City'.

Packed with people

Rio is a very crowded city. Over six million people live here. These include some of the country's richest people who live in large, luxurious mansions in the city's suburbs. However, over a quarter of Rio's entire population live in tiny shacks in the favelas which line the city's hills. The people who live here are very poor. Most have very badly paid jobs or do not have any work at all. Many survive by begging. There is a lot of crime in the favelas.

Tourist attractions

Many thousands of tourists visit Rio every year. There are many attractions in Rio, including two long, sandy beaches called Copacabana and Ipanema. People visit the beaches to sunbathe and to play beach sports. The city is overlooked by a mountain called Sugar Loaf Mountain. A cable car runs from the city to the mountain top. From here, you can enjoy views of the city and the sea from 396m up. There are also exciting boat rides out to sea to go fishing and sightseeing. Alternatively, you can take a trip from Rio to visit the Amazon rainforest and the Pantanal.

I live in Rio. I get up around 7.30am, have breakfast and then do homework for the rest of the morning. In Brazil, we go to school for just four hours a day. Some children go in the morning, but I go in the afternoon. At 11.30am I have lunch with my mum. She then takes me to school. We have lessons in Portuguese, maths, English and other subjects. My favourite lesson is art. My mum picks me up from school at 5.30pm. We have a long holiday from school between December and January.

Marissa

Farming in Brazil

About a quarter of the population in Brazil are farmers. As you travel around the country you'll see many vast plantations. Most of the food grown is sold abroad rather than eaten by the Brazilian people. Nearly all of the country's good farming land is owned by just a few rich landowners. People who live on small family farms often struggle to make enough money.

Brazilian ranchers sometimes use long horns to call to each other as they round up their cattle.

Brazilian farmers use tractors to work their fields.

Sugarcane

If you travel through north-east Brazil, you will pass huge fields filled with what look like giant grasses. This is sugarcane. The sugar we put in drinks or on cereal is made from this. Brazilian people also grow sugarcane to make ethanol, a fuel used to run cars. Most cars in Brazil run on a mixture of petrol and ethanol. Other crops, such as coconuts and bananas, are also grown in the north-east.

Soya and cattle

In the centre of the country, where areas of rainforest have been cleared, plantations of soya are grown. Soya is sold throughout the world where it is used to produce cooking oil and animal feed. To the south of the Amazon, large areas of the Brazilian Highlands are used to raise herds of cattle. Brazil is a major producer of beef.

Once they have been picked, coffee beans are sieved to remove soil, twigs and leaves.

Coffee and oranges

A large variety of different crops are grown in the south-east, including cotton, tomatoes and **manioc**. There are also vast plantations of coffee and orange plants. Brazil is one of the world's leading producers of both coffee and oranges. In the far south of the country there are huge vineyards where grapes for wine are grown. Most of the country's wine is produced in this area.

Food and drink

As you travel around Brazil, you will taste many different dishes. Each region has its own cuisine, but the meals are usually made up of one or more of the same basic ingredients, including beef, pork, fish, shellfish, beans, coconut, lime and rice. People from many different countries have settled in Brazil over the years, and so Brazilian food is now a mixture of many different styles of cooking, such as Amerindian, African, Portuguese, Italian, German, Spanish and Asian. In recent years, foreign foods such as hamburgers, pizza and sushi have also become popular.

Rice and shellfish with spicy sauces are popular dishes.

My name is Rodrigo. I live in Teresina in north-east Brazil. I like to eat arroz e feijão (rice and beans) and acarajés, which are deep-fried cakes made from black-eyed beans. My friend Leila lives in Manaus in the north of Brazil and she eats alligator meat. She says it's really tasty. Sometimes we visit friends in Cuiaba in the centre of Brazil. They live near a cattle farm. They like to eat churrasco, which are grilled meats served on a metal skewer, a bit like a barbecue.

The national dish of Brazil is feijoada, a mixture of pork, black beans, spices and rice. It is served throughout the country and is usually eaten at lunchtime.

These men are fishing the waters of the Fernando de Noronha National Park, a group of 21 islands over 350km off the coast of Brazil.

Fish

Brazilians eat a lot of fish and seafood. Fishing takes place along the country's coast, which is one of the longest in the world. Fishing is also done up and down the Amazon River and in the Pantanal swamp area in the west of Brazil. Cod and shrimp are two fish favourites. They are cooked in a seafood stew called mariscada, with mussels, squid and clams.

Fruits

Brazil grows a wide variety of tropical fruits, such as bananas, melons and mangoes. The fruit is sold at local markets and at huge city-centre supermarkets, many of which are open 24 hours a day.

Watermelons are sold whole or by the slice in Rio's food markets.

Having a party!

Every year, Rio de Janeiro has the largest street party in the world, known as Carnaval (the Portuguese word for carnival). People decorate beautiful floats, dress up in colourful costumes and dance the **samba** through the streets. Carnaval lasts for four days just before **Lent**. In Catholic countries, such as Brazil, Lent is the time when people give up things they enjoy most, such as music, dancing and eating nice food. Carnaval is an excuse to enjoy all these things together for one last time. Smaller, local carnivals are also held throughout Brazil at this time.

Samba schools

Rio has a special area known as the Sambódrome – a narrow arena with space for up to 100 000 spectators – where the largest and most colourful parades and parties take place. These are put on by the city's samba schools, which spend all year practising their dance moves and preparing their costumes. Many thousands of people come to watch the procession and dance along to the samba music. Samba schools help to provide jobs for the local community, with many people getting paid to work as dressmakers and carpenters on the floats.

At Carnaval time, thousands of people fill the streets of the Sambódrome.

Giant floats

During the Carnaval, spectacular floats are paraded through the streets. Floats are usually decorated to look like a Brazilian historical event or legend. They are always very colourful and may have special effects, such as a dragon with wings that flap and holes that belch smoke. On the top of the float sits someone dressed in a very elaborate and expensive costume. Millions of people watch Carnaval on television throughout Brazil.

It can take up to a year to make a Carnaval costume.

My name is Beatrice. I live in the Barra da Tijuca neighbourhood of Rio. Every week our samba school meets at our quadra, or samba court. A samba school is not the sort of place you go to learn things, like a real school. It's more like a club. We go to practise our dance moves and to help make the costumes and floats for the next Carnaval. All the neighbourhoods in Rio have a samba school, even the poor ones. Samba schools give jobs to local people.

Carnaval floats have lots of things to see on them. They are always very colourful.

Football mad

Football is by far the most popular sport in Brazil. You'll see people playing it everywhere – on football pitches, on the streets, even on the beach. Thousands of fans go to watch their favourite team. Every four years, millions of Brazilians sit around their TVs to watch the progress of the national team in the FIFA World Cup. If a very important match is being played, such as the final, lessons are sometimes cancelled so that school children and teachers can watch the game.

The famous Brazilian footballer Pele scored over 1000 goals in his career – a world record.

During the World Cup, football fans paint their faces the colour of the national team.

A successful sport

Brazil is the only country to have won the World Cup five times, in 1958, 1962, 1970, 1994 and 2002. The country has produced some of the most famous players of all time, including Ronaldinho, Ronaldo, Romario and Pele. Many people believe Pele is the best player of all time.

The Brazilian player, Rivaldo, lifts the World Cup Trophy after the 2002 tournament.

Here, Brazilian children are playing football on the beach, using coconuts for goalposts.

Different games

People play several different types of football in Brazil. As well as the standard sort of football played on a grass pitch, Brazilians also play beach football and 'footvolley'. This is a combination of football and volleyball in which the players have to kick a ball over a net.

YOU'VE GOT MAIL

When we're not playing football (which we do a lot), my friends and I like to play basketball or, if it is really hot, go swimming. Sometimes we also play a traditional Brazilian game called Queimada, which is a bit like 'tag' or 'it' and is played by two teams. What do you play?

Estevan

Industry and power

Brazil has changed a lot over the last few years. Sixty years ago there were not many industries and the country imported most of the goods it needed from abroad. Since then, Brazil's economy has grown enormously. It now has lots of successful industries which produce a range of products including cars, planes, clothes, shoes and electrical equipment. Brazil is the richest country in South America and has the ninth-largest economy in the world.

Hydroelectric power

Brazil gets over 90 per cent of its electricity from hydroelectric power (HEP). HEP is made by building a dam across a river, which creates a large, artificial lake. The force of the lake water passing over **turbines** in the dam creates power, which is turned into electricity. The Itaipu Dam in the Paraná River in western Brazil is the world's largest dam, and the world's largest producer of HEP.

Vast amounts of water pass through the country's dams every day, producing a lot of electricity.

Brazil has many large factories, such as this timber mill on the Jari River.

Julieta's school essay

The Brazilian currency is the real, you say it ray-al. (reais is plural). In the early 1990s my country had very high inflation. Inflation means that things keep getting more expensive. In 1993, inflation had reached 5000 per cent. This meant that something which cost just one real at the start of the year, would cost 5000 reais at the end of the year! In 1994, new notes and coins were issued and prices were brought back down. Fifteen years ago, it was common to have banknotes of mil reais (1000 reis) or even conto de reais (one million reais). Now they don't exist. My parents said that it took people a few weeks to get used to using the new coins and banknotes.

Pollution

Having a successful economy and thriving industries creates jobs and brings money to Brazil, but it also creates problems. Forests are cut down to make room for mines and factories. Harmful chemicals are sometimes released into rivers where they kill fish. In the city of São Paolo, where many of Brazil's biggest industries are located, the air is becoming very **polluted** because of all the smoke and fumes being belched out by the factories.

In some parts of Brazil, the forest has been cleared to provide timber and make room for new factories.

Activity ideas

1 Plan an imaginary trip around Brazil. If you could pick six places to visit, where would you go? Why? How would you get to Brazil? How long would it take? How would you get to the different destinations in Brazil? If you could visit just one place in Brazil, where would it be?

2 Find out more about rainforests. Brazil has the largest stretch of rainforest in the world. Use your local library and the Internet to learn about other rainforests around the world. What makes a rainforest different from other types of forest? What other countries have rainforests? What animals and plants live in these areas? Using an atlas, trace a rough outline of the countries of the world onto a piece of paper. Using coloured pencils, colour in all the areas of rainforest. What do they have in common?

3 Make a 3D picture of the Amazon rainforest. On a sheet of card, draw the rough shape of a section of forest, showing the flat forest floor, some tree trunks (also known as the understorey), the canopy (the tree tops) and the emergents (one or two very tall trees that stick out above the canopy). Tear up strips of brown paper to make the fallen leaves of the forest floor and glue firmly in place. Crumple up some green paper to make the canopy and glue in place. Paint the trunks with brown paint. Using the Internet, research which animals live where in the rainforest – such as ants on the forest floor, jaguars in the understorey, howler monkeys in the canopy and parrots in the emergents. Print out pictures of these animals, cut them out and stick them in place on your picture. Finally, label your picture.

4 Research and write a project on poison arrow frogs that live in the rainforest. What are they? How did they get their name? What colours are they?

5 Using books and the Internet, make a fact file about the Amazon River. How long is it? How many different rivers flow into it? Where does it start? Where does it end? What animals and plants live in and alongside the river? What do people use the river for?

6 Search through cookery books and on the Internet to find recipes for some Brazilian dishes, such as acarajés or feijoada. With an adult, cook the food and eat a Brazilian meal. You could also buy some examples of different Brazilian foods to sample. Write reviews of the food. How do they compare to British foods? Make a display of the reports.

NOTE FOR ADULTS: Please ensure that children do not suffer from any food allergies before making or eating any food.

7 Brazil shares a border with ten other countries. Using geography books and the Internet, make a fact file about these different countries. What are their capital cities? What languages are spoken there? What are their currencies? How do they differ from Brazil?

8 Research and write a report comparing and contrasting life in a rainforest village with life in a Brazilian city.

9 Using travel brochures and websites, find the images and pictures of Brazil most often shown to tourists travelling to the country. Print out the pictures to make a collage of 'Tourist Brazil'. What are the most popular tourist destinations in Brazil? What ideas and images do travel websites use to sell Brazil as a place to go on holiday?

10 Find out where the ancestors of the people who live in Brazil came from. Who were the first people to live in the country? Why have people come to live in Brazil? Draw a world map and mark the different countries people have come from to live in Brazil.

11 Using an atlas, find other places around the world on the same **latitude** as São Paolo, Brazil's largest city. Find out if the average temperatures are the same, or if they differ. Plot the results on a chart to compare the temperatures in the different countries.

12 Imagine you are travelling right around Brazil, passing through a number of cities, along the Amazon River and through the rainforest. Write entries in an imaginary blog about your journey. What do you see? Who do you meet? What do you learn about Brazil?

13 Write a tourist leaflet describing a city in Brazil. What does the city look like? What sort of buildings does it have? Is it on the coast or inland? What fun things can people do there? Remember to use persuasive language to encourage people to visit.

14 Carry out research using the Internet and books to find out more about the Itaipu Dam in western Brazil, which is the world's largest dam and also the world's largest producer of hydroelectric power (HEP). What are the advantages and disadvantages of HEP? What is the environmental impact? Is using HEP better or worse than using fossil fuels? Use your information to hold a debate with friends or classmates for and against HEP.

15 Find out more about the samba. Listen to some recordings of samba music by Brazilian musicians. What sort of music is it? What instruments do the musicians use? What sort of beat does it have? See if you can learn some basic samba dance steps.

Glossary

açai A small Brazilian fruit.

carbon dioxide A gas in the air around us. Plants and trees 'breathe' by taking in carbon dioxide and giving out oxygen.

campaign To do certain actions – such as protesting to a government – in order to achieve a certain aim.

climate change When the weather pattern changes over a number of years – it may become hotter, colder, wetter or drier.

conservation groups Organizations which try to protect the environment.

continent A large area of land which contains many countries, such as South America.

extinction When an entire species of animal or plant dies out.

FIFA World Cup A competition held every four years between international football teams. The winners are awarded a trophy known as the World Cup.

global warming The raising of the Earth's temperature by the release of gases, such as carbon dioxide, which trap sunlight.

humid Moist or damp.

indigenous People, animals or plants who were the first to live in a place.

industrial To do with the manufacture of products.

latitude Distance from the equator (an imaginary circle around the middle of the earth, shown on most maps).

Lent A forty-day period in the Christian religious calendar beginning on Ash Wednesday and ending at Easter.

leukaemia A disease which affects blood and bone marrow.

manioc A type of root vegetable common in Brazil.

migrated travelled from one area or country to live in another. People who migrate are known as migrants.

mixed race People whose parents are from different racial backgrounds.

plantations Very big farms where usually one crop, such as coffee, is grown on a large scale.

polluted When something becomes impure because it is full of harmful chemicals.

rainforest A type of hot, wet jungle.

region An area of a country or continent.

resorts Special places where tourists can go on holiday.

samba A fast, lively dance from Brazil.

silt Tiny bits of rock and earth carried along by a river.

slums Areas of poor, cheap housing.

species Types of animal or plant.

suburbs The outskirts of a city where people live.

swamp land An area of very wet ground.

temperate Weather that is neither very hot nor very cold.

tributaries The smaller streams and rivers that feed into a large river.

tropical A hot and humid climate.

turbines Engines that spin.

Index